A Prayer for Today

"Fresh Insights"
on
The Prayer of Jabez

Bob Gass

Synergy Publishers
Gainesville, Florida 32635

All scriptures are taken from the King James Version unless otherwise noted.

Other Bible Translations used as noted:

TM	–	The Message
NIV	–	New International Version
NLT	–	New Living Translation
LB	–	Living Bible
AMP	–	Amplified Bible
NKJV	–	New King James Version

A PRAYER FOR TODAY
ISBN 1-931727-03-1
Library of Congress Catalog Card Number: Pending
Copyright ©2001 by Bob Gass
P.O. Box 767550
Roswell, GA 30076

Synergy Publishers
Gainesville, Florida 32635

TABLE OF CONTENTS

✣

"Jabez was more honorable than his brothers,

and his mother called his name Jabez, saying,

"Because I bore him in pain."

And Jabez called on the God of Israel saying,

"Oh that You would bless me indeed,

and enlarge my territory,

that Your hand would be with me,

and that You would keep me from evil,

that I may not cause pain!"

So God granted him what he requested.

1 Chronicles 4:9-10 (New King James Version)

Acknowledgements

The Prayer of Jabez, Wilkinson, (Multnomath)

God's Inspirational Promise Book, Lucado, (Word)

The Uncommon Minister, Murdock, (Wisdom International)

Overcoming the Enemy, Jakes, (Albury Publishing)

God's Little Devotional Book Class of 2001, (Honor Books)

Motivation to Last a Lifetime, Engstrom, (Zonderman)

The 21 Most Powerful Minutes in a Leader's Day, Maxwell (Nelson)

Note: Italics found in the Scriptures used in this book, are placed there by the author for emphasis.

INTRODUCTION

One day my friend, Guy Morrell, called and said, "Bob, have you heard of the little book *The Prayer of Jabez?* It was written by a fellow called Wilkinson. I believe he lives somewhere near you in Atlanta."

I laughed and said, "I know him, we met years ago when he was a guest on my daily television show *The Breakfast Club.* He's Founder of *Walk Through The Bible Ministries,* one of the finest daily Bible guides in the world. And I'll tell you something even more interesting, three years ago, when we began publishing our daily devotional, *The Word For You Today,* here in the States, it was *his* staff that put it together for us and got it ready for press. I've never worked with a better group of people."

"Do yourself a favor," Guy said, "Go out and buy a copy!"

I did!

Few books have blessed or impacted my life more. I understand why millions have read it and are now praying the prayer of Jabez every day.

I pray it myself each day! I also encourage others to pray it too, and see what happens.

The thoughts that follow were sparked, in large part, by reading Bruce's book.

"Mike," I said, "If you want what Jabez had,

you've got to do what Jabez did!

His prayer was backed up

by a lifestyle of obedience to God."

A Prayer For Today

1

HELP, THE PRAYER OF JABEZ ISN'T WORKING FOR ME!

One day, Mike, a friend of mine, told me his whole family had read *The Prayer of Jabez,* and were praying it every day.

"Do you pray it too?" I asked. "I did for a while, then I quit," he said. "Why?" I inquired. *"Because it didn't work for me; nothing happened."*

Now Mike's a bit of "a wheeler-dealer." He buys old houses, fixes them up, turns them over, and makes a quick profit. He also does the same with cars. And not a week goes by that he doesn't buy at least a dozen Lottery or Powerball tickets, hoping for that one-in-eighty-million long shot of becoming an overnight millionaire.

As I listened to him I wondered, "Does he actually *think* that if he just prays a four-line prayer every day, his problems will disappear, doors will open, and money will pour out of heaven?"

This man Jabez, who suddenly stepped out of the Old Testament, sold millions of books, stayed at the top of *The New York Times Best Seller List,* and became a household word, prayed for *four things.*

His short, but life-changing prayer, is recorded in Second Chronicles, Chapter Four, and verse ten (NKJV). Here are the four things he prayed for:

(1) *Greater success:* "Oh, that you would bless me indeed ." (2) *Greater influence:* "…and enlarge my territory." (3) *Greater power:* "…that your hand be with me." (4) *Greater protection:* "…and that You would keep me from evil, that I may not cause pain."

And the Bible says, "So God granted him what he requested" (1Ch 4:10 NKJV).

So why wasn't it working for Mike?

Because God's promises come with *conditions.* He didn't read the fine print. In this "microwave mentality" generation, we risk turning the prayer of Jabez into a get-rich-quick formula, or a way of manipulating God to get what we *want,* instead of taking the time to ask Him what we *need.*

Before you pray for prosperity, pray for purpose, because God won't finance self-indulgence. Success without character can derail you, or even destroy you! The examples are all around us.

The truth is, you can pray this prayer till the cows come home, and if your motives are selfish, God won't answer it. James writes, "When you ask, you do not receive, because you ask with wrong motives, that you may spend what you get on your pleasures" (Jas 4:3 NIV).

A few weeks later I saw Mike in Starbucks coffee shop. As we shared a cappuccino, I decided to take up where we'd left off.

"I've been thinking about what you said,"

I began.

"Thinking about *what?*" he asked.

"Didn't you say the prayer of Jabez wasn't working for you?"

"Yep," he told me, "And probably a lot of others too."

Looking at him squarely, I said, "Mike, if you want what Jabez *had*, you've got to do what Jabez *did*. His prayer was backed up by a lifestyle of obedience."

"What are you taking about?" he asked, as he dipped a biscotti in his coffee.

"I think I've figured out why the prayer of Jabez works for some and not for others. Got a few minutes?"

"Absolutely," he replied.

"As a devout Israeli," I began, "Jabez would have been a tither. Actually, the thought of *not* giving God the first tenth of his income, would never have occurred to him."

Mike laughed, "Here comes the commercial."

"No," I said, "You want the Jabez blessing? Let me show you something."

That day I happened to have with me, *The New Living Translation* of the Bible, so I started reading, "Bring all the tithes into the storehouse… If you do…I will open the windows of heaven for you. I will pour out a blessing so great you won't have enough room to take it in. Try it! Let me prove it to you!" (Mal 3:10 NLT).

While he was still processing that, I turned quickly to the Book of Matthew and said, "In case you think tithing was just something they did in the Old Testament, listen to what Jesus said. 'You are careful to tithe even the tiniest part of your income, but you ignore the important things of the law – justice, mercy, and faith. *You should tithe*, yes, but you should not leave undone the more important things'" (Mt 23:23 NLT).

I could tell by his expression that tithing as a pre-condition to blessing, hadn't once crossed

Mike's mind.

"And let me show you something else," I said, turning to Deuteronomy, "Jabez would have grown up hearing these words on a regular basis. Listen, 'You will experience all these blessings *if you obey* the Lord your God'" (Dt 28:2 NLT).

"Mike," I said, "God *cannot* bless you beyond your last act of disobedience."

Then I pointed him to certain verses in the chapter I'd carefully underlined, and began reading, "You will be blessed…wherever you go, both in coming and in going…your enemies …will attack you in one direction, but they will scatter from you in seven. The Lord will bless everything you do…the world will see you are a people claimed by the Lord, and they will stand in awe of you. The Lord will give you an abundance of good things…The Lord will make you the head and not the tail, and you will always have the upper hand" (Dt 28:1-13 NLT).

Clearly, Mike liked what he was hearing.

"Now let me show you something *else* that will keep this prayer from working for you," I said, turning this time to Psalm Chapter 66, verse18. "If I had not confessed the sin in my heart, the Lord would not have listened." (NLT)

"But we all sin and make mistakes," Mike countered, "So based on your line of reasoning, this prayer won't work for *anybody.*"

"No," I responded, "This scripture simply means, if you refuse to acknowledge your sin and seek forgiveness, God won't answer your prayers. He can't! If He did, He'd be violating the very conditions He Himself laid down in His Word.

"You see, the most important thing in my life is *my confidence before God.*"

"Your *what?*" he asked.

"Any time I can't figure out whether or not I should get involved in something," I replied,

"I just ask myself one question. How will this affect my confidence before God, especially when it's time to come before Him in prayer? That question *never* fails to lead me in the right direction."

Mike was listening intently.

"Read this scripture to me," I said, handing him my Bible. Adjusting his glasses, he began to read 1 John 3, verses 21-22 (NLT). "Dear friends, if our conscience is clear, we can come to God with bold confidence, and we will receive whatever we request, because we obey him and do the things that please him."

"It's not a four-line prayer that brings God's blessing," I said. "It's a four-line prayer, *backed up by a lifestyle* that pleases God!"

As we left the restaurant that day, and walked toward our cars, I said, "Mike, it's not praying for what *we want* that brings God's blessing, but having the confidence that we're praying according to what *He* wants for us. He *already* has a plan in place for us. The trouble is most of us have no idea where we are in His plan, so we ask for things *now,* that He hasn't scheduled until *later.* (And in some cases, not at all.) You see, you can pray for a roof till you're blue in the face, but if your foundation hasn't been properly laid you won't get one, because you don't need one yet."

"Good point," He answered.

As Mike opened his car door to get in, I said, "Got time for one more thought?"

"Sure," he replied.

Turning to Hebrews Chapter 10, I pointed him to these words, "...Continue to do God's will. *Then* you will receive all he has promised" (Heb 10:35-36 NLT).

Putting my hand on his shoulder I said, "Mike, God knows the where's, the when's, and the how's of blessing you. You can trust Him to know *what* you need, *when* you need it, and *how* to get it to you. Okay?"

"Okay," he said. Then hugged me, got into his car, and drove off smiling.

"Discover what God says about you,

then refuse to believe anything different.

After all, when you've got God's opinion,

what difference does anybody else's make?"

2

Remove the Label

I was named after my Uncle Robert, my dad's oldest brother. But names in the Bible were prophetic. They were given to indicate your *destiny*. Now since the name Jabez means, "pain maker," his family obviously didn't think he was going to amount to much, or make the world a better place.

The trouble with labels is, if we accept them, they limit us. They keep us from dreaming, or believing in our inherent, God-given potential.

Jacob the patriarch didn't know *who* he was until God told him.

His parents called him Jacob, which means *"deceiver."* But it's a label God never intended him to wear, and a destiny God never intended him to fulfill. So God changed his name to Israel, which means *"a prince with God."* (Ge 32:28). Note those words, "with God." What you are with men is not nearly as important as what you are with God.

If you are looking at your shortcomings, and wondering how God could *love* you, much less *bless* you, read these words:

"Do you think anyone is going to be able to drive a wedge between us Christ's love for us? There is no way! Not trouble, not hard times, not hatred, not hunger, not homelessness, not bullying threats, not back-stabbing, not even the worst sins listed in Scripture" (Ro 8:38 TM).

No matter how unworthy you may feel today, you cannot shut off, stop, or in any way diminish the flow of God's love toward you. Nothing can change the way He feels about you. Nothing can alter the fact that He's going to continue to love you no matter what you do or say.

Never lose sight of that, because God's love will: (1) Heal your emotions. (2) Cause your self-esteem to grow. (3) Put a foundation of worth and dignity under you. It's what allows you to respect yourself!

It'll also motivate you to discipline yourself. And that's important, for when you truly *value* something, you want to protect it and develop it.

Paul writes, "It's in Christ that we find out who we are "(Eph 1:11 TM).

Read your Bible and discover what God says about you, then *refuse* to believe anything different!

The negative messages you received, and the perceptions of worthlessness you formed about your self in childhood, where wrong *then,* and they're wrong *now.* They're wrong because God says so. Listen, "For I know the plans I have for you, says the Lord. They are plans for good and not for evil, to give you a future and a hope" (Jer 29:11 TLB).

Throw out the old tapes! They simply don't apply anymore. Learn to forgive yourself, accept yourself, love yourself, and believe in yourself.

God does!

Paul adds, "*We belong* to his dearly beloved son" (Eph 1:6 NLT). Once you understand that God *already* accepts you, the acceptance of others will become a lot less important.

Don't misunderstand me, you won't become uncaring or unmoved by people. On the contrary, you'll become more caring and more deeply moved by their needs – because now your own are being met by God!

The fact that God accepts you transforms your prayer life.

Once you realize that you have a *direct* pass to "the throne room," you'll stop trying to talk God into hearing you. You'll realize that you can come to Him at any time, knowing that you'll always be received with love and concern no matter where you are, or what's going on. He'll hear you because "you belong."

Once you really grasp that, your self-esteem will begin to rise, you'll refuse to wear the labels others have put on you, and your reluctance to approach God with either your sins or your requests, will vanish.

Why? Because you're loved! You're accepted! Nothing and nobody can ever change that!

"You don't have to do anything
to earn God's love,
but you do have to do certain things
to experience His blessing!"

3

"Oh, that you would bless me indeed."

A PRAYER FOR GREATER SUCCESS

God *delights* in your success. He *wants* to bless you. What good parent wouldn't?

That may come as a shock, especially if you grew up hearing that God isn't interested in you having material things, or enjoying temporal success. Maybe you were told that He likes you to be poor, so you'll be humble, or needy, so you'll be more dependent on Him.

But if we've barely enough to get by on ourselves, how can we help anybody else?

God told Abraham, "I will bless you…*and you will be a blessing*" (Ge 12:2 NIV). God doesn't mind us having money, He just minds money having us. Money is called "currency" because it's supposed to flow *through* us, and bless others.

The blessing of God made Abraham the

most successful businessmen of his day. Had he lived now, he'd probably have been on the cover of *Fortune Magazine*. And how about Joseph? The blessing of God made him second only to Pharaoh, in all of Egypt. Think you could use a little of *that* kind of blessing?

One of the most significant things Bruce Wilkinson does in his book, is to point out our need for a new definition of the word "bless." We've taken something as big as the Atlantic Ocean, and reduced it to the contents of an Aspirin bottle.

When somebody sneezes we say, "Bless you." A minister stands at the end of a church service and pronounces "a blessing" over us, but by the time we get to the parking lot we've forgotten it, because the truth is, we can't remember any difference it ever made in our lives anyway!

The words "bless you" have become synonymous with, "Have a nice day."

Nothing could be further from the truth!

The word *blessing* means, *"supernatural favor."* It's not something ethereal that occurs only in a religious atmosphere; or futuristic, that happens only when you get to heaven.

There are three things you need to know about the Jabez blessing: (1) It's for "the here and now." (2) It's for every area of your life. (3) It's something God, and God *alone* can give you.

As I recall it, the church I grew up in seemed to preach against everything; especially money! And it worked. Because by and large, people with money never attended. And God help the ones who did!

I'm convinced that more than once, when someone of means dropped in, our pastor would change his text from, "God so loved the world," (Jn 3:16) to, "Go to now, ye rich men, weep and howl for your miseries that shall come upon you" (Jas 5:1). With just a handful of people in the congregation, there wasn't much doubt *who* he was taking aim at.

Once I remember him declaring, "When you see all those rich people on the other side of town with their big houses and their big cars, do you think they're *really* happy?"

Now my mother, the most devout Christian I've ever known, happened to be sitting beside me, so I didn't dare say what I was thinking, which was, *"You bet your life they are!"*

So, how did I learn what I know today about the blessing of God?

By listening to the *people* He sent into my life. They introduced me to a God who *longs* to bless His children, so that they, in turn, can *be* a blessing to others.

But I was also afraid. I'd heard so much about "The prosperity Gospel," and the excessive lifestyles of those who preached it, and I wanted no part of it.

It took me several years to arrive at what I now know. But little by little, as I read my Bible and prayed for understanding, God began to show me scriptures I'd read before but never really understood, because either I "spiritualized" or "futurized" them. Here are a few:

"Do not let this Book of the Law depart from your mouth; meditate on it day and night, so that you may be careful to do everything written in it. Then you will be prosperous and successful" (Jos 1:9 NIV).

"Walk in his ways, and keep his decrees...so that you may prosper in all you do and wherever you go" (1Ki 2:3 NIV).

"And God is able to make all grace abound to you, so that in *all* things, at *all* times, having *all* that you need, you will abound in every good work" (2Co 9:8 NIV).

"I am the Lord thy God which teacheth thee to profit, which leadeth thee by the way that thou shouldest go" (Isa 48:17).

"The blessing of the Lord brings wealth" (Pr 10:22 NIV).

"Command those who are rich in this present world...to put their hope in *God, who richly provides us with everything for our enjoyment.* Command them to do good, to be rich in good deeds, and to be generous and willing to share" (1Ti 6:17-18 NIV).

Then God gave me an opportunity to experience His blessing first-hand. It happened one week after the Oklahoma City bombing.

My ministry, which was much smaller then, had been carrying a $23,000 debt for several months, and try as I might I couldn't seem to catch up.

At the time I was preaching in a small church in northern Ohio, and at the end of the Sunday evening service, the pastor handed me a check for $2,000. I said, "Thank you." Immediately a voice within me said, "That's not for you!" In a conversation that nobody but God and I were aware of, I replied, "But my name's on it." The voice said, "No, it's for Mrs. Martinez."

Then I remembered.

Just a few days after the blast, a friend called to tell me about a Spanish pastor named Gilbert Martinez, who worked with street-people in Oklahoma City. On the morning of the bombing, he'd taken two men to the Murrah Federal Building to sign them on for government assistance, and help them find work.

They arrived three minutes before the explosion. All three were killed.

Gilbert Martinez left a wife and five children: the youngest, only two weeks old. I remember being very moved at the time, but as so often happens, I got busy and forgot about it.

One week later, a voice within me was saying, "Send this $2,000 to Mrs. Martinez."

"How do you know it was *God* speaking to you?" Because I would never have told myself such a thing, given the financial situation I was in!

I tried to bargain. Ever do that? I reminded

God of my debt, and that I needed to apply every penny I could get toward it.

But God was silent.

Then I tried a different approach. "Would it be okay if I sent $1,000 and kept $1,000?" I said, hoping to strike a compromise.

Again, no answer.

I've discovered that before God will issue you *further* instructions, He'll wait to see what you do with the last ones He gave you.

Feeling the pressure I said, "Lord, how would it be if I sent $1,000 right away, then $250 a month for the next four months?"

As clearly as I've ever heard it, God's voice said to me, *"What's in your hand right now won't meet your need; what's in mine will. Which would you like?"*

I remember thinking, "I never had it explained to me so clearly before."

Looking back, I now realize, God was giving me an opportunity to move to a *new level* of blessing.

If I hadn't given the $2,000, would God have loved me less? No! You don't have to do anything to earn God's love, but you do have to *obey* Him, to experience His blessing.

Up until then, the largest amount I'd ever given to God's work in a lump sum was $1,000. Now God was stretching me. He was teaching me that if you want something you've never *had*, you've got to do something you've never *done*.

Finally I said, "Yes Lord, I'll do it!"

"How did you feel?" you ask. Hopeful! I said to my wife, "I hope this works!"

Three months went by and nothing happened. I'd meet the mailman in the morning, hoping for a miracle. I'd shake hands with my friends and wonder, "Has God been speaking to you lately?"

Those were the longest three months of my life!

During that time, God brought to my attention the law of sowing and reaping, specifically these words by the Apostle Paul: "He who sows bountifully, will also reap bountifully" (2 Corinthians 9 NKJV).

Giving is like sowing a seed; when God receives your seed, He schedules your harvest. That's why Paul also wrote: "Be not weary in well doing: for in due season we shall reap, if we faint not" (Gal 6:9). God reminded me several times during that three-month period, that the "due date" on my harvest was coming, and not to doubt Him, or speak words which contradicted Him.

Then one morning as Debby and I were eating breakfast at Murphy's Restaurant in downtown Atlanta, a waitress came to our table and asked, "Is there a Reverend Gass here?" I raised my hand. "You've got a phone call," she said.

It was my administrative assistant, Tom Lissak. "Can you come to the office right away?" he asked. "There's something you need to see."

When we arrived half-an-hour later, he handed me an envelope with an Australian post-mark. Inside it was a check and a letter from a lady I'd never met, or even talked to. As best I can recall, she'd attended a conference in Melbourne, at which I'd been a speaker, and purchased some of my teaching tapes.

The letter said she'd received an inheritance of $230,000, and that God had wakened her three nights in a row, saying, "Send a tithe to Bob Gass Ministries."

And she did!

That morning I held in my hand the largest check I'd ever received in the mail – $23,000!

The following day a check for $5,000 arrived from some friends in New York. In twenty-four hours God had provided us with $28,000 and wiped out the Ministry's entire debt.

That was a turning point in my life! Every year for the next five years, God doubled our ministry's outreach and income.

When you start praying, "Oh that you would bless me indeed," get ready for instructions; and for the ride of your life!

But you need to understand something.

You can't just ask for God's blessing, then sit in the seat of "do nothing," and wait for it to drop into your lap. No, the Bible says, "It is he [God] that giveth thee power *[ideas, ability, creativity]* to get wealth, that he may establish his covenant" (Dt 8:18). Notice the words "to get," sometimes you've got to go out and get it!

When God gives you the ability to succeed, it usually begins as an *idea*. It only becomes a reality when you make a plan and carry it out. Otherwise your seed rots in the ground of excuses.

Never laugh at somebody with an idea, for ideas come from God. After all, if God's our creator, and we're made in His likeness, shouldn't we be creative too?

Some of the world's most successful people

got to where they are because they'd a better idea for cooking chicken, or writing a computer program.

The *gift* God gave you is your key to success! He didn't give it to you to be put on display, wasted on worthless things, or denied out of a false sense of humility.

No, he gave it to you to be *invested.*

Jesus told the story of three men who were each given money to invest. The first two doubled theirs. The third, because he wasn't a risk-taker, buried his in the ground because he was afraid of losing it. As a result, Jesus called him, "a wicked, lazy servant" (Mt 25:26 NIV).

Look out! *Fear* is one of your greatest enemies. It numbs your spirit and incarcerates your creativity.

Use what God's *already* given you! Stop praying for oak trees, while acorns are lying all around you. Your ideas are the tiny acorns from which great oaks grow.

"Why don't we pursue God's blessing more aggressively?" you ask. For a lot of reasons.

Some of us grew up believing that if we asked God for *more,* it meant we didn't appreciate what we already *had,* or that we were "worldly," or immature, or discontent.

Or maybe we think we're too old!

If *you* are in that group, listen: "The righteous will flourish like a palm tree…they will still bear fruit in old age, they will stay fresh" (Ps 92:12,14 NIV). Do you know that a palm tree produces the *greatest* harvest in its final years? Often God keeps the best to the last!

The truth is, there is no magical age at which excellence emerges, or success suddenly comes. With God you're never too young or too old to be blessed, and to in turn bless others.

Thomas Jefferson was 33 when he drafted *The Declaration of Independence.* Charles Dickens was 24 when he began *The Pickwick Papers,* and 25 when he wrote *Oliver Twist.* Newton was 24 when he formulated the law of gravity.

On the other hand, Verdi was 80 when he produced *Falstaff.* Goethe was 80 when he completed *Fauste.* Tennyson was 80 when he wrote *Crossing the Bar,* and Michelangelo was doing some of his finest work at 87.

Seize the day! Redeem the "now" moments of your life. The age you're waiting for may *never* arrive.

Don't allow your lack of education, your ethnic background, your subservient position, or your poor wages, to keep you from asking God for greater blessing.

There's a story in Second Kings, Chapter Five, about *a cleaning lady* who reached out to a five-star general, and introduced him to a God who could heal him of his leprosy. Take a moment and read it, because there are two important lessons in it for you:

(1) There's a purpose in your being where you are! This lady wasn't in the general's house just

to make beds and clean toilets; she was there by divine appointment. Instead of complaining, start looking for somebody who needs what God's given you. Think: all of your life can be training for one moment, one crisis, or one opportunity. Peter writes, "Always be prepared" (1Pe 3:15 NIV).

(2) *What a difference a day can make!* Yesterday she was a nobody, today she's a gift from God, and the most popular person in the house. The world focuses on big names, but when they've run out of answers and out of hope, God says He'll pour out His spirit upon His "handmaidens" (Joel 2:29). When He does, people who normally "wouldn't give you the time of day," will suddenly be interested in what you have to say, because you're in the right place, at the right time, with just the right word.

Keep renewing your mind and strengthening your faith. Pray, "Oh that you would bless me indeed," then start *expecting* great things from God.

And keep listening – you can never tell when the Divine Conductor will give you your cue.

"When you leave this world,

your material possessions will go to others.

The only thing that will remain is ...

your influence."

4

"And enlarge my territory."

A Prayer for Greater Influence

The second line in the prayer of Jabez, is a request for more territory, or *greater influence.*

John Maxwell says, "During your lifetime you will directly, or indirectly, impact the lives of at least 10,000 other people."

The question is – *"How,* will you impact them?"

When you leave this world your material possessions will go to others; the only thing that will remain is your *influence.*

At the end of a life well lived, the Apostle Paul wrote, "I have fought a good fight, I have finished my course, I have kept the faith" (2Ti 4:7). Having said that, he handed the ministry over to Timothy, walked to the executioner's block, and was thereby relieved of his duties.

Yet his *influence* is a million times greater today than it was when he penned those words in a Roman prison cell. The thirteen books he wrote, have changed history and become part of the World's number one best seller – the Bible!

Here's a line worth pondering from one of his books: "He [God]…had designs on us for glorious living" (Eph 1:11 TM).

What kind of living is that? Living with impact! Influencing the world around you! Not just making a *living*, but making a *difference!*

In the movie *Rain Man*, Dustin Hoffman plays a savant – someone, who in a sea of disabilities; has an island of genius. In the film, he's incredibly gifted with numbers. Other savants have amazing abilities in art and music. The truth is, *all* of us arrive equipped and empowered to do something special. You have within you an island of genius. God's given you a gift! Believe it! Discover it! Develop it! Cherish it! Use it! Give it away! *That's* "glorious living!"

And money – or the lack of it – doesn't necessarily determine your life's impact.

People entrusted with fortunes, have lived, died, and made little or no difference at all. Yet others, short on material things but long on vision and compassion, have made the world a better place for all of us.

Consider the influence of a *schoolteacher.*

A sociology class conducted a study of 200 young people from Baltimore's inner city. It concluded, "Not one of them has a chance for success." Twenty-five years later, a sociology professor doing a follow up study, located 180 of the original 200 subjects. Of that number, 176 had become doctors, lawyers, ministers, and successful business people. When he asked each of them to explain the success they now enjoyed, they all pointed to one teacher.

The professor found that teacher and asked her what she'd done to make such an impact on them. She simply smiled and said, "I loved them, and they knew it!" No wonder Paul writes, "Love *never* fails" (1Co 13:8 NIV).

Consider the influence of an *athlete*.

For months Eric Liddell trained with his heart set on winning the 100-meter race in The 1924 Olympics. Most sports writers predicted he'd win. At the games, however, he learned that the race was scheduled to be run on a Sunday. That posed a major problem for him, because he didn't believe he could honor God by running on the Lord's Day, so he bowed out of the race. His fans were stunned. Some who'd praised him, now cursed him. He came under intense pressure, but he stood firm. Then something happened: a runner dropped out of the 400-meter race, which was scheduled on a weekday, and Liddell offered to fill the spot. This really wasn't "his race," because it was four times longer than the one for which he'd trained. Even so, he ran, won it, and set a new world record.

Not only did he earn an Olympic Gold Medal; he also made an uncompromising stand for his faith in the process.

Eric Liddell went on to become a missionary to China, where he eventually died in a prisoner-of-war camp. Even though he never lived to see it, he impacted millions of people, who went to see the 1981 Academy Award winning movie of his life, *Chariots of Fire*.

Consider the influence of a *parent*.

As a child Ruth Simmons told one of her classmates, "Someday I'll be a college president."

That was remarkable coming from the twelfth child of Texas sharecroppers. Little did Ruth know that it would be the presidency of Smith College in Massachusetts, the largest liberal arts college in the nation. She's the first African-American woman to head a top-ranking college. Since female presidents, especially black ones, are rare, let's explore what happened.

Most success stories begin with parents. In this case the emphasis is on her mother, who stressed the importance of hard work. Ruth says, "I worked hard at everything I did. And not necessarily because I was interested in good grades, or looking for praise. No, I worked hard because that's what I was *taught* to do."

Peter Rose, a member of the college search committee said, "We wanted to cast the widest possible net, for the best possible person. What convinced us that she was the right person for the job, was her work ethic, her strong academic performance, and the force of her personality."

In his great book, *What the World Owes to Christians,* Dr. Victor Pierce, an Oxford scholar, shares the stories of people who've changed the way we live. Here are the stories of a few, and the gifts they gave us.

Anesthesia. How would you like to be operated on without anesthesia? That's the way they did it, until a Scottish doctor named James Young Simpson, introduced something called "artificial sleep."

As a student at Edinburgh University, he was attracted to surgery because he was troubled by the pain and the mortality rate experienced during operations. As a result of reading Genesis 2:21, *"And the Lord God caused a deep sleep to fall upon Adam,"* Simpson thought chloroform might be the answer.

He first experimented on himself.

Finally, in 1847, the first three operations with chloroform took place. One of the patients, a young soldier, enjoyed it so much that he seized the sponge and inhaled again. "It was too good to be stopped," he said.

At first Simpson encountered opposition. Some thought it was a sin to interfere with nature. "Hand me the Bible," said Dr. Simpson.

"This is how God operated on Adam." He made speeches, wrote letters and pamphlets, and tried to convince those who opposed him, that this was the way forward. In a setback, when three deaths attributed to Chloroform were reported from other hospitals, Simpson was able to show them that they were not applying the anesthesia correctly.

The tide turned when Queen Victoria gave birth to her eighth child under chloroform, and declared that she was, "Greatly pleased with its effect."

Bicycles. The bicycle revolutionized village society. This is revealed in church parish registers, where the names of those locals joined in marriage, were eventually integrated with names from further afield. Why? Because people were now cycling from village to village, and town to town. Until this time families were very in-bred. Needless to say, their health improved greatly as a result of the bicycle.

But who invented it? An English clergyman by the name of Reverend C.W. Penny. He gave the world the first penny-farthing bicycle and tri-cycle.

Braille. In 1824 Louis Braille, another Christian, invented a system of raised dots on paper so that blind people could read. What a wonderful enlargement to their world that was! He invented sixty-three symbols, to represent every language in the world, thereby enabling God's Word to be placed in the hands of the visually impaired, for the first time.

Typewriters. The typewriter radically changed the commercial world, and was a forerunner to the modern word processor.

But how come a Christian invented it?

It was invented to write sermons! I'm not joking. Christopher Sholes was concerned about his pastor, who'd been busy all week visiting the victims of an epidemic, comforting the bereaved, and conducting funerals. Consequently, he had no time to write his Sunday sermons.

One day Sholes, discussing with a friend what could be done about this, said, "It seems a pity there ain't some quick method of writing for busy folks like parsons." His friend replied, "Why not invent a machine?" "I'll try," responded Sholes.

That rainy afternoon was the beginning of months of hard work. Finally a group assembled one day to see him tap out on paper, in capital letters, the words, "C. LATHAM SHOLES, SEPTEMBER 1867."

Six years later the Remingtons recognized the typewriter as "Something that could revolutionize business."

In those days clerks were mostly men. But the *Young Women's Christian Association* started offering courses in typing for women. Initially it created a scandal, but as the first typists to be trained were women, employers rushed to hire them.

Hence, the typewriter and the YWCA determined that a woman's place was not only at home, but could also be in the office!

Communications. You owe the convenience of your cell phone and your computer, to a Christian named Samuel Morse, the dash-dot-dash inventor, who gave us Morse code and communication between Continents. Our most sophisticated forms of communication are largely due to some of his discoveries.

What a different world it was before him. First class news took two weeks to reach the USA, and news of a major victory could take as long as six weeks to reach Britain.

One day a friend said to him, "I say, Morse, when you were experimenting, did you ever come to an absolute deadlock, not knowing what to do next?" "More than once," replied Morse. "What then?" asked the friend. Morse shared a secret. "I did something of which the public knows nothing. I got down on my knees and prayed for light, and light came. And when my inventions were acknowledged by flattering honors from America and Europe, I said, 'Not unto me, O Lord, not unto me, but unto Thy name give the glory.'"

That's why the first message ever be transmitted by transatlantic cable read: "What God has wrought."

Add to this growing list another Christian named *Louis Pasteur*, the French scientist, who showed us that infection is the result of things we can't see, namely germs and viruses. He introduced sterilization methods, which ultimately saved the lives of multitudes.

And how about *William Booth*, founder of The Salvation Army, who when he was too old

A PRAYER FOR TODAY

and sickly to attend their general conference, sent a telegram consisting of one word – a word that brought all the delegates to their feet – *"Others!"*

But the record would be incomplete without one more name: *William Wilberforce,* the man who gave his life to abolish slavery.

History records that in one thirty-day period in 1814, his efforts produced 1,500,000 signatures protesting slavery, which he then presented in Parliament. He was constantly under threat from slave owners, not to mention those Members of Parliament, who themselves owned plantations and slaves.

Encouraged by people like John Wesley and Prime Minister, William Pitt, Wilberforce awakened the conscience of the nation.

One of the greatest influences in Wilberforce's life was his friend, John Newton, author of *Amazing Grace,* himself a former slave-trader, and now a vicar.

On his deathbed in 1833, Wilberforce received the news that Parliament had finally passed The Act of Abolition, outlawing slavery forever.

Good ideas are great – *God* ideas are even better!

You see, what God initiates He backs up with the resources of heaven. Paul said, "My God shall supply all your need according to his riches" (Php 4:19). According to *what?* Imagine being empowered by God, and underwritten by His resources!

God's problem has never been a lack of ideas. It's finding people who'll leave their comfort zone and act on them. People like Abraham, who "By faith…when called to go…went, even though he did not know where he was going" (Heb 11:8 NIV). And how did he end up? By fulfilling the promise, "All the nations of the earth will be blessed through you" (Ge 28:14 TLB).

"But is it okay for me to pray for more business?" you ask.

Yes! God wants to bless *your* business, so that you can help to carry out *His;* which is the business of reaching the world with the Gospel.

Usually God only gives us His ideas when: (1) ours have failed. (2) We've laid aside all our pre-conditions and are willing to do whatever He says. (3) We're prepared to risk. (4) We're committed to giving Him all the glory.

Stop despising the things that make you unique. You were born at just the right time, in just the right place, with just the right gifts, to fulfill a plan that *nobody* but you can fulfill.

King David acknowledged that when he wrote, "You saw me before I was born and scheduled each day of my life..." (Ps 139:16 TLB).

If you want to have *greater impact* for God, pray this prayer:

"Lord, it's taken me a long time to figure out that I'm different by divine design; that You've made me with abilities, traits, and a genetic combination that nobody else has. Nobody in all the ages of time has ever been me – and nobody ever will. Deliver me, Father, from feeling weird; from wishing I were someone else. Deliver me from envy and jealousy toward others. Help me to discover the unique person You created me to be; to enjoy the little things that make me so special; so one-of-a-kind. *Help me to realize that I was born to make a difference; to give this world something no one else can give. Amen."*

"Anything done in my own strength

will fail miserably…

or succeed even <u>more</u> miserably."

5

"That your hand would be with me."

A PRAYER FOR GREATER POWER

God has a habit of calling us to do things, which are *so far beyond* our natural ability, that if He doesn't empower us or intervene on our behalf, we'll fail for sure.

The Bible is a "David and Goliath" book. It teaches us that *every* act of God in our lives is designed to increase, not decrease, our dependence on Him. He'll never give us an assignment, which does not require His direct participation. If you can do it without God, it's not *of* God.

And Jabez knew that!

That's why he prayed, "Lord when I'm successful, keep me dependent on you! Don't let me get out of balance! Help me to keep first things first!"

If you think getting to the top is tough,

you'll quickly discover that the real challenge is *staying* there, and maintaining your spiritual and emotional health in the process!

In the Bible, God's right hand represents *power.* Joshua told the Israelites, "The hand of the Lord is powerful" (Jos 4:24 NIV).

Jabez understood that the more successful you are, and the more influence you have, the *more* you must rely on God. And that's tough on our egos!

When I preached my first sermon at thirteen, I dreamed of one day being like Billy Graham and speaking before great crowds. I smile as I look back. Clearly God had a different plan in mind for me.

In those days I'd pray anxiety-ridden prayers like, "Lord, if You can't use me, take me out of the way! I'd rather be dead than fail." Each time I approached the pulpit I felt like my life was on the line. I'm glad my congregation didn't know how unqualified I felt, or how scared I was.

My second pastorate was in Bangor, Maine, which I thought at the time, was as far northeast as you could get, and still be in the will of God.

Often I'd walk through the darkened sanctuary in the wee hours of Sunday morning, having studied to the point of exhaustion. I'd lay hands on each seat, ask God to fill it, and the person who sat in it. In tears I'd look up and pray, "Lord, empower me. Give me *Your* words, otherwise I'm just recycling the thoughts of men."

If anybody on earth was less qualified for this job than me, I'd wanted to meet him.

My education in Belfast, Ireland, finished at age fifteen, and I didn't have the privilege of attending either college or seminary. As a result, I struggled for years with terrible feelings of inadequacy.

During my first year in Bangor, I learned from Archie Parrish, minister of evangelism at Coral Ridge Presbyterian Church in Florida, how to win souls using the *Evangelism Explosion* method. As insecure as I was in the pulpit, I was even more fearful one-on-one.

I hadn't a clue how to build a successful Sunday School, so I read a book by a Baptist pastor called Dr. Jack Hyles. He'd built a Sunday school of 20,000 by bussing kids in from government housing projects. So I rented twelve buses and began doing the same thing.

Sometimes our bus-workers would actually have to go into an apartment where the father and mother had been out drinking all night, wash the children, dress them, and put them on the bus. On the way to church, they'd feed them milk and donuts.

The entire twelve years I was there, I felt like I was "flying by the seat of my pants." Basically I still live that way. The only difference is, *now* I know whose power is keeping me airborne!

To my amazement and God's glory, when I left Bangor, the church had become one of the largest in northern New England.

Today I write a daily devotional, which is read by over a million people, in nineteen languages.

How did *that* come about?

Well, for the last thirteen years I've served on the board of United Christian Broadcasters, an organization committed to pioneering national Christian radio in the United Kingdom and Ireland. At present, the law there prevents that. You can be licensed to play rock, rap, rave, or reggae, but not Christian music.

As I understand it, the *Radio Authority* is concerned that if they open the door, American broadcasters will invade the airwaves. Or worse, if they license one particular group, that group will either proselytize, or offend those of other faiths.

So until now, the door has been closed to everybody.

United Christian Broadcasters International,

the parent organization, has built over one-hundred-and-sixty stations in places like Russia, Estonia, New Zealand, Australia, and the Islands of the Pacific. Still, the British government has resisted all attempts to change their law.

But we're not discouraged. It took *seventeen* years before the law was changed in New Zealand. Today that country is the *first* in the British Commonwealth to have its own national network, with over sixty-four stations. And the wonderful thing is, *Radio Rhema,* has proven to be a blessing and a force for unity in the country.

So how do you get your message out when you can't use the airwaves? You've guessed it – the printed page!

Seven years ago I wrote the first edition of *The Word For Today.* (In America and Canada it's called *The Word For You Today.*) We published 3,000 copies and gave it away to anyone who wanted one.

Today in the UK, we publish over 500,000

copies, and one out of every three churches uses it, making it Europe's most widely read daily devotional. Up to 10,000 letters a week come in to our offices in Stoke-on-Trent, England, telling us of lives changed, and people blessed through reading it.

Now, humanly speaking, it's impossible to write something *six months in advance* that will meet the needs of people all the way from the Australian outback to the Brooklyn Bridge, and from a daily newspaper column in Hong Kong to the quiet, scenic villages of the U.K. and Ireland.

That's why I pray every day, "Oh…that your hand would be with me."

It has been said, "When you walk by faith to the edge of your ability and step into the dark, God will do one of two things: either He'll put solid rock beneath your feet, or He'll teach you to fly!"

Every day I become increasingly aware, that *He* is the wind beneath my wings!

Don't you think that's what Paul was driving at when he wrote: "Not that we think we can do *anything* of lasting value ourselves. Our only power and success comes from God?" (2Co 3:5 NLT).

Ted Engstrom tells of a man on a cruise ship, who rescued a girl who had fallen overboard. At a party given in his honor that night, he gave the shortest "hero speech" ever made. "Ladies and gentlemen," he said, "I just want to know one thing – who pushed me?"

You may smile, but the truth is most of us aren't naturally courageous. We need a push!

Robert Flood writes, "We like to think of ourselves as a mixture of Davy Crockett, John Wayne, and the prophet Daniel, when the truth is we're more like Gulliver, tied down by tiny strands of fear, real or imagined, and the result is a tragic loss of courage."

And being a Christian doesn't exempt you.

Listen to these words, "Jesus went before

them…and as they followed, they were afraid" (Mk 10:32).

Max Lucado writes, "Before they were stained-glass saints on the windows of cathedrals, the disciples were next door neighbors trying to make a living and raise a family. They weren't cut from theological cloth, or raised on supernatural milk. They were just an ounce more devoted than they were afraid, and as a result, they did extraordinary things."

Someone has estimated that, three-hundred-and-sixty-five times, the Bible says, "Fear not." That's one for every day. Why? Because each time you do the thing you fear to do, fear loses its hold over you, you become a little stronger, and a little more dependent on God.

And that's how He planned it!

"The more you have,

the more you have to lose,

and the busier you are,

the more you have to fight to maintain

your walk with God."

6

"And that you would keep me from evil,
that I may not cause pain."

A PRAYER FOR GREATER PROTECTION

John Basagno, Pastor of First Baptist Church in Houston, Texas, told a friend, "When I was called to preach at twenty-one, my father-in-law told me that only *one* out of *ten people* who enter the ministry, will still be in it by the time they reach sixty-five."

He continued, "I've written in my Bible the names of twenty-five friends who went to Bible College with me. Twenty have already dropped out." Then, looking earnestly at his friend, he said, *"I'm fighting hard to be one of those who make it. I want to finish well!"*

A strong start is important, but it doesn't guarantee a strong finish.

What happened to the nine out of ten who

didn't make it? They were the ones who said, "I've done enough growing, exercised enough discipline, taken enough advice, dreamed enough dreams, and set enough goals. Now I'm taking it easy."

At age seventy the Apostle Paul wrote, "I run straight to the goal with purpose in every step...otherwise, I fear that...I myself might be disqualified" (1Co 9:27 NLT). There is no "safe age," and no harbor free from storms, except in the arms of God.

And Jabez knew that – that's why he prayed, "...keep me from evil, that I may not cause pain."

Take a look at Samson. He started strong, yet he ended up losing his vision, his freedom, his influence, this power, and ultimately his life. What happened?

(1) *He broke the rules!* The relationships he formed destroyed him. The bible warns, "Be ye not unequally yoked together with unbelievers" (2Co 6:14). An ox and a donkey may both be

God's creatures, but they can't sleep in the same stall or work in the same harness. Why? Because their *natures* are different! When God says "No" to certain relationships, he's not being difficult, He's being protective. Heed Him!

(2) *He lived by his impulses!* He thought he was in love, when he was simply in heat! When confronted about his choices, he replied, "She pleaseth me well" (Jdg 14:3). Before it was over he'd become a laughing stock. Peter writes, "Abstain from sinful desires, which war against your soul" (1Pe 2:11 NIV). Learn to live by your principles, not your impulses.

(3) *He misused his gift!* Samson used his God-given strength for personal gain. Listen to these words, for they characterize his life: "Then shall ye give me" (Jdg 14:13). God gives us gifts to fulfill *His* purposes, not *ours*. When we misuse them we always end up in trouble.

(4) *He was blind to his weaknesses!* You may not like to believe that your private imperfec-

tions will have public consequences, but you can't escape what you are.

Jabez prayed, "Keep me from evil" because he realized that the more you have, the more you have to *lose,* and the busier you are, the more you must *fight* to maintain your walk with God.

On Colorado's *Long Peak* lie the remains of a giant 400 year-old tree. Age, storms, and avalanches couldn't bring it down. What did? A tiny beetle you could crush under your foot. It ate right through the bark and devoured its heart.

Solomon says it's "The little foxes that ruin the vineyards" (SOS 2:15 NIV). *Little* attitudes, but if you practice them long enough they become fixed attitudes. *Little* indulgences, but if you give place to them long enough, they desensitize you to sin.

Remember when certain things bothered you? Now they don't even give you a second thought. That's because we're being systemati- cally desensitized by the culture around us!

Before a moral problem got out of hand in the Corinthian Church, Paul attacked it head-on. Listen, "One of your men is sleeping with his stepmother. And you're so above it all, that it doesn't even faze you!…You pass it off as a small thing, but it's anything but that. Yeast, too, is a 'small thing,' but it works it way through the whole batch…get rid of this 'yeast'" (1Co 5:1-7 TM).

Why does God make such a big deal of this? Because sin hurts us, and anything that hurts one of His children makes Him angry.

Jabez prayed for protection, because he understood that the greater the assignment, the greater the attack!

Israel never fought any battles in the wilderness, but when they entered The Promised Land they encountered thirty-one kings who had to be dealt with, and seven nations that had to be conquered, if they were going to possess it.

The devil is not going to send you a

congratulatory telegram because God's blessing you. No, every chance he gets he's going to attack you in: (a) any area of frustration; (b) any area of vulnerability; (c) any area that's unfocused or undisciplined.

"But I'm not even sure I believe in an actual devil," you say.

He'll be glad to hear you say that, for he does his best work in the dark! His most successful strategy is *denying* his own existence, thereby enabling him to operate with complete freedom in your life.

Get real! If satan attacked Jesus three times, do you think he's going to give you a free pass? He *always* attacks those who are in line for God's blessing.

A few years ago, Dr. David Youngi Cho, Pastor of the world's largest church, spoke to 1,000 pastors in Buffalo, New York. They'd come to hear the man from Seoul, Korea, who'd built a church of 800,000 members, and learn his secrets.

His opening remarks left them speechless.

As he walked to the pulpit he introduced a member of his staff by saying, "This man travels with me wherever I go. You see, like all men, I too am susceptible to sexual temptation, and he is my safeguard."

That's the kind of honesty that will keep you safe, strong, and help you to fulfill your God-given assignment.

Paul writes, "Put on the whole armor of God, that ye may be able to stand" (Eph 6:11). Notice the words, "That ye may be able to stand." The armor is God's; the stand is yours!

God's armor is strictly for those who are willing to stand for what's truly important; like the salvation of your family, the success of your marriage, your walk with God, and *anything else* that's important to you. The message is clear; suit up, stand up, and hold your ground!

Pay particular attention to Paul's words in

Ephesians 6:17: "And take...the sword of the Spirit, which is the word of God." The sword referred to here is a large dagger used for fighting at close range.

Understand this clearly, you'll have to stand toe-to-toe with your enemy. To defeat him you'll need to know how to use the Word of God, which Paul describes as, "Living...sharper than any double-edged sword, it penetrates...it judges the thoughts and attitudes of the heart" (Heb 4:12 NIV).

God's Word can determine with pinpoint accuracy what's going on in your life.

When you come face-to-face with the devil, it's the *only* weapon capable of rendering him powerless.

If you're serious about living "the blessed life," the best advice I can give you is, have a set *time* each day for meeting with God, and let *nothing* keep you from it.

Why do I feel so strongly about this? You'll

find the answer in these two scriptures:

(1) "And as long as he sought the Lord, God made him to prosper" (2Ch 26:5). (2) "But when he was strong, his heart was lifted up to his destruction" (2Ch 26:16). Those two statements define the rise and fall of Uzziah, one of Israel's greatest kings, and they serve as a warning to us today.

Dr. Mike Murdock says, "What you do daily, determines what you become permanently." He's right! David the Psalmist writes, "Every morning, I tell you what I need, and I wait for your answer" (Ps 5:3 NCV).

But is it really necessary to spend time with God *early* in the morning?

Any moment spent with God can change you; but don't you think it's smart to plan your trip before you take it? Why start your day without a sense of His direction and peace? Is any voice more important than His, or more reliable?

If you're struggling to rise early and pray, start doing three things:

Set an achievable goal. Don't focus on getting up an hour earlier, try fifteen minutes. You can always add to it. When you set impossible goals you create memories of failure, instead of memories of success.

Learn how to enter His presence. Listen, "Come before his presence with singing" (Ps 100:2). God loves music. He responds to worship and singing. Music can actually lift your spirits and dispel your fear. When King Saul was depressed, we read, "David took an harp, and played...and the evil spirit departed" (1Sa 16:23). Try it!

Educate those around you concerning your new prayer time. Few things are more impacting that watching a person with a consistent prayer life. Without saying a word, you'll challenge those who don't pray, and thrill those who do. They may even want to join you.

Some years ago I preached in Tallinn, Estonia. While there I reconnected with an old friend called Mart Vahi.

This remarkable man has helped build over eighty churches, a Bible school, and put an FM Christian radio network on the air that covers two thirds of the country.

On Sunday morning I spoke to about 1,000 people in his church. The building we met in was the former Communist Party Headquarters. When I gave an invitation for people to come to Christ, twenty people came forward. The last, was an attractive young woman with blonde hair.

After leading them in a prayer of commitment, I directed the altar workers to take the new converts to a room for further counseling.

As Mart and I stood side by side in front of the podium, the girl with the blonde hair came by, shook Mart's hand, and asked him, "Do you remember me?" Before he could answer, a counselor led her away.

Clearly shaken, he turned to me and said, "Now I remember!"

And this is the story he told me:

"When the Russians annexed Estonia, thousands of my country men were sent to forced labor camps in Siberia, where they died and were buried in unmarked graves. Families were still grieving and wounds needed to be healed.

"So, when the Iron Curtain fell and Estonia declared its independence, the new government decided to take a plane load of officials, including a clergyman, into Siberia, to hold a committal service for the Estonians who'd died there.

"I was invited to go along and officiate.

"When it was over, we all linked arms around a bon-fire and sang patriotic songs. As we stood warming ourselves and celebrating the rebirth of our country, a young woman with blonde hair slipped her arm through mine. At first I thought nothing of it. Then I realized that I was being propositioned!

"She was very attractive, the wife I loved was far away, and a voice within me whispered, 'Why not?'

"I couldn't believe I was having such thoughts.

"In that moment the temptation was so strong, I broke free from her grasp and ran back to my cabin. There I got down on my knees, asked God for strength, and thanked Him for making a way of escape for me.

"The following morning, a very hung-over official of the Estonian Government, told me how he'd spent the night "partying" with a bottle of Vodka and an attractive blonde."

Five years later, that *same* blonde-haired woman came walking down the aisle of Mart's church in response to my altar call.

Looking at me intently, Mart Vahi asked, "Bob, what if I'd given in? What would have happened to our churches, our Bible school, our radio stations, or the work of God in this country?"

When you pray for greater success, greater influence, and greater power, don't forget to pray for *greater* protection: "...keep me from evil, that I may not cause pain."

✣

"The Prayer of Jabez, gives us a new concept of

God! Not God the auditor, before whom

our books never balance, or God the judge,

in whose eyes we never measure up,

but instead, God our loving heavenly Father,

whose nature, whose will,

and whose desire, is to bless us...

and bless us with 'Life in all its fullness.'"

John 10:10 (NLT)

7

"So God granted him what he requested."

MAKING IT WORK FOR YOU

Recently I talked to a publisher in New Jersey about printing two new books for me. "Have your heard of *The Prayer of Jabez?*" I asked him. *"Heard* of it?" he replied, " We're getting ready to print it. The demand is so great, it's taking several publishers just to keep up with it!"

Multitudes are now praying the prayer of Jabez each day, and experiencing a level of blessing they never dreamed possible.

Who are these people?

People who are tired of settling for less, and want more, so they can do more for God.

People who have discovered that you can exchange *your* lack, for *God's* provision.

People who've come to understand that certain blessings are given only when you *ask* for them, and ask in faith believing.

People who realize that God's blessing brings supernatural favor, that enriches *every* aspect of your life.

People who are willing to make their wants, subservient to God's will.

People who believe that God knows *what* we need, *when* we need it, and *how* to get it to us.

People who've come to understand that when you pray according to the will of God, the windows of heaven open, and His blessing pours into your life.

People who understand that if you don't *ask,* you won't get all you're supposed to have. Actually, you'll forfeit those blessings that come *only* when you do. James says, "You do not have, because you do not ask" (Jas 4:2 NIV).

The truth is, The prayer Jabez prayed gives us a *new concept of God.*

Not God the auditor, before whom our books never balance, or God the judge, in whose eyes we never measure up. But God, our loving heavenly Father, whose *nature,* whose *will,* and whose *desire,* is to bless us, and bless us with "life in all its fullness" (Jn 10:10 NLT).

Paul writes, "Now to him who is able to do immeasurably more than all we ask or imagine, *according to his power that is at work within us*" (Eph 3:20 NIV).

There's the key!

Recognizing that God, the God who formed the universe, *is within us, working through us daily* as we engage our minds, open our mouths, move our feet, and use our hands to do what He has *already* put into our hearts.

It's understanding that He never stops calling us to take one more step, do one more thing, or engage in one more act of faith.

It's keeping pace with Him, knowing that His direction is always right, His timing is always perfect, and His results are always best.

"Why does The Prayer of Jabez work?

Because when you pray for greater <u>blessing</u>,

greater <u>influence</u>, greater <u>power</u>, and

greater <u>protection</u>, you're praying

in the perfect will of God,

and asking Him for…

<u>exactly</u> what He <u>wants</u> you to have!"

8

A FINAL THOUGHT

I'd like to challenge you to *add* to your daily prayer life, the prayer of Jabez.

When you do, it'll change what you *expect* from God, and what you *experience* each day. You'll start to see Him working in your life – even in the smallest details – because now you'll be *looking* for Him.

But I must emphasize two things without which the prayer of Jabez simply won't work.

First, be humble! The Bible describes the call of God as "the high calling," (Php 3:14), yet the higher your calling takes you, the lower you must become in your own eyes.

Jesus said of John the Baptist, "There is not a greater prophet" (Lk 7:28). Yet John said of Jesus, "He must increase, but I must decrease" (Jn 3:30). When the Lord called Ezekiel to be His voice to the nation, Ezekiel felt so inadequate that he fell to the ground and God had to say to him, "Stand upon thy feet, and I will speak unto thee" (Ez 2:1). When John the Revelator came face to face with Christ on the Isle of Patmos, he wrote: "I fell at his feet as dead" (Rev 1:17).

The more successful your are the more humble you must be, and the more you must acknowledge that the power that works in you is not *human* ability, but *God's* ability.

None of us know exactly what the "thorn" in Paul's life was, but we know *why* he had it. He tells us, "Lest I should be exalted…there was given to me a thorn in the flesh" (2Co 12:7).

Thorns come in many forms. God customizes them to our personality and designs them according to our need. *Your* thorn may be a problem child, a turbulent marriage, a stubborn habit, or a life-long affliction. It's what deflates you when others try to exalt you; it's what enables you to receive a compliment and not become arrogant.

In one sense it's not a thorn, it's a thermo-stat, regulating your attitude, keeping you on your knees, and reminding you that God is your source – and God alone!

Second, be consistent. Start praying the prayer of Jabez today, and continue for the next twenty-one days. If you do, you'll find it easy to pray for the rest of your life. That should be your goal!

Write this prayer out and tape it on your bathroom mirror, or some place where you'll be reminded to pray it each day!

Begin to keep a record of the *changes* and the *miracles* that take place in your life, as a result of praying it.

Try to be more sensitive to the *doors* God opens, and the *people* He sends across your path, either to bless you, or be blessed by you.

Get an extra copy of this book for your friends and family members. Don't keep "the Jabez blessing" to yourself.

Why does The Prayer of Jabez work?

Because when you pray for greater *blessing,* greater *influence,* greater *power*, and greater *protection* – you're praying in the perfect will of God, and asking Him for *exactly* what He wants you to have!

New Books by the Author:

ISBN: 1-931727-04-X

ISBN: 1-931727-02-3